The biography

of

broken things

by sean Thomas dougherty

Mitki/ Mitki

Charlotte, North Carolina
Columbus, Ohio

Also by Sean Thomas Dougherty:

Except by Falling

The Body's Precarious Balance

Love Song of the Young Couple, the Dumb Job

The Mercy of Sleep: Poems and Drawings from the Saint Catherine of Siena Project

Sunset by the Chain-Link Fence

One Nation Under a Groove: Selected Poems 1990-1998 (Audio)

Mitki/Mitki Press
P.O. Box 570
Denver, NC 28037
http://www.mitkimitkipress.com
publisher@mitkimitkipress.com

ISBN 0-9707802-3-0

Book design and layout by Jeff Parker.
Cover photo by Suzanne Proulx.
Printed and Bound in the United States of America.
This book is printed on acid-free paper.

Some of these pieces, in different versions, were published or are to appear in
the following places: *Grain, A Quarter After Eight, Xavier Review,* and the an-
thologies *Illuminations* (2001 Plymouth State College Writer's Group) and
Short Fuse: Global Fusion Poets (2002 Rattapallax Press). The author thanks the
editors of these publications.

Thanks to Keith Gilyard for the line *to leap from a ledge of language.* "the hu-
man hum" is for Arielle Greenberg.

"For Decades" appears as "At a Certain Hour. On a Certain Day" in *Except by
Falling* (2000 Mesa State College) and on Jolie Christine Rickman's CD *Suffer
to Be Beautiful* (2000 Hen Records).

The degree to which we can resist certain narratives
depends upon how we are able to rewrite them.
—Peter McLaren

Now you might say...don't write in the transparent
modes...But nevertheless, I feel sometimes I ought to
speak in a way that a larger number of people here and
there might be interested in; you might not just have the
converted, but those on the line, etc.—by bringing in a lot
of things that are efficacious, in the sense of a rhetorical
poetry...
—Jackson Mac Low

My brothers turned to me and said:
"You are not Jewish. You do not go to the synagogue."

I turned to my brothers and answered:
"I carry the synagogue within me."
—Edmond Jabes (trans. Rosmarie Waldrop)

I had a complex about getting too complex.
—Talib Kweli of *Black Star*

In the biography of broken things

In the Diaspora of *come froms*. In the burning threads of be-
cause. In the olive branches of a small girl's hands combing
her hair as if all of history's been gutted. In the collapsing
querulous bodies' mute speech. In the bus stations of com-
pulsory *destinudo*. In the philosophy of coffeehouses, *who
cares*. In the simple annoyance of a crowd of strangers, *how
come*. In the alleyways of sudden longing, there is a river: the
good intentions of others, *a how come not hurrying*. Who
cares what the living make as to whether? —here is your testa-
ment. *Who cares* what eyes the green flies have sewn shut?
Swear there is a camellia and a sharkfin in the handshake of
anywhere. In the accidental that leads to well founded any-
thing. The re-assembling of someday as if *Amens* of the hu-
man hum.

Write me a recipe for the holy longing that the night glides in, for the light that falls through badly hung curtains, for somebody calling you. Write me a recipe for rain swept streets, for that feeling of loss when the train pulls out of the station, for a childhood that cures disillusionment. Write me a recipe for fruit stands. Write me a recipe for porch rockings, for a solo of sunlight falling on blue silos, for laundry flapping from a tenement line. Write me the recipe for a language emancipated as the wind, that pollinates the familiar with the disavowal of meaning in our day, and at the same time teaches us to tie our shoes.

The first evening of the fallen snow, the television flickering its insomniac light. Jackie Robinson at the roots overworked sometimes when I was a child I subscribed to most of Marx's theses but the disharmonies were noticeable about man's potential as something which takes longer exists just as we must struggle without hope Abbie Hoffman wrote before he died, trees cooing *Thy brother is come, and though Father has killed the fatted calf.* At the back of the bus they are plotting the overthrow of Genghis Khan, who with Saint Gertrude is planning on attending the Great Dance. Look at his tassels twirling! The falling snow is covering my block with a fine sand of silence, a sad eyed icon of a white woman walks passed, she is Ahkmatova searching for her child, she pushes an empty stroller, she is wearing all black. On her shoulder I witness the angel siphoning off the living, she is too tired to wrestle as did Jacob, she is too tired to seek for aught the assurance that Suso sought, *Could I kill a pretty baby that smiled at me? No, no I would rather suffer every trial that could come upon me!* Orthodox priests in full dress, their large hats rising out of a convertible. Is this the same question of representation you were going to ask— how could you know the living from lime? Why should we believe what you see when we know there is nothing you can claim infernal outside of one's shoes, *the signification of one's shoes?* Am I nothing but eyes from a window, am I more than a theory when greeted we one another we theorize through what we see, what *They say*— we must always listen with something beyond our ears— I am more of this, more than language, through it I am feed, I am fought. Laughter, wakings, smilings, music. Is the knife used? Each of them a form of human self-activity leading us to the camps or to a community of freedom?...I am my body, but my body is not you.

There is laughter and laundry outside—my neighbor is drunk again, his name is Michael: arch angel, winged one, he wears a hat pulled low over his ears, he is around fifty, he is a lost cause, he dreams of small things, moments away from his wife. Leslie is a large powerful woman, I hear her yelling at him "I do everything around here"—from what I can tell, she is right, left at the corner, she is walking holding the hand of their eight-year-old daughter, her infant-son on her hip, I see her always carrying something, carrying bags of groceries, carrying laundry, carrying bags to and from their old rusted station wagon, her arms are thick, they sway from her sides like sausages, she can be vicious and gentle in the same step—once I saw her swat her daughter to the ground at the same time cradling and comforting the child.

Hope and apocalypse, the binary at the beginning from which all well waters spring, the underground rivers, railroads, emancipation, proclamation, proclivities, programs. Programs spring from hope and fear, the two threads, the two misgivings, The Old Word and The New, each Epoch enters, leans its heavy shoulder toward one or the other. These disjunctions, progress, regress, two steps forward two steps back, sunlight on the sidewalk, children playing hopscotch. I picture Lenin, the metaphor, he is in prison reading Chekhov. It is snowing. It is always snowing when I read the Russians, when I think the Russians, saint Doestesevky, no. Human, hard hands, eyes that scanned the streets, Mayakovsky's fallen horse. I dream of Stalin in his study, how he couldn't see his own hands for the fear of the space in between them. There is nothingness all around, the emptiness of space, time, trembling old woman on the subway, the lights flickering, I am four, five, my mother's hand holding mine, the first time I am frightened—of what. I love the rocking, like water, the womb I would think years later, the blue light we ride, Death enters, he wears a broad hat, he wears rings on his fingers, he has come from a black wedding, flies buzzing, the horse is trying to raise its head, it is trying to raise its head, get up Mayakovsky is calling, get up, get up, each time its hooves slip on the black ice, he is us Mayakovsky is thinking, here on a cold street, such shoulders, such power, yoked by the shoulders, the quick lashes, he is trying to raise his head, his bulbous eyes reflecting the faces, and he falls, he falls, he is flying.

he is flying

Along the Detroit river with Pete Markus, we watched three cranes rise into the gray sky, their legs making the last three letters of the alphabet, he laughed. Driving back through the industrial section, we counted boys on the corners with beepers, leaning on poles, stopped when we reached forty-three. Forty-three seconds to go. Counting Crows on the radio, bad Pop band. *In the old country*, Pete said then, *to count crows was to count the death of dreams.*

to count the death of dreams

There is a hillside in old Moldavia where my dead are buried
before the children sleep, they are breaking bread, they are
singing and writing poems in Yiddish, they are reading the
Talmud, they are thanking. There is a Northern Irish village
the last rebels are plotting in the dim light of a barn, they are
making bombs out of Kerosene and Grace, Parnell is still
alive, the priests are plotting his demise, in the Belgium Congo
a thousand slaves have died in the mines in the moment it
took for a man named Seamus to run his finger along a fig-
ure of rifles shipped—to count, to count the figures, figures,
as in human figures, figurative, statues (dictators, the dead),
stature (hierarchy), the figures (numbers), the forgiven, the
imprisoned, the old women, the villages, in the hillsides, the
numbers do not show them before the soldiers enter the vil-
lage, the children, the women, men in the mud, they are
laughing, they are gathering hay.

they are gathering hay

A fragment, steam in the coffee pot, diner, Northern Massachusetts, outside Worchester, Pepe is walking from work, in the window the woman watches, her husband is snoring, he has broken his ankle, Pepe is arriving to fill in at the mill, the weaving loom, the world is watching, black crows on the power lines, phone calls you walk down the halls to make, in the shining cities, before the wind creeps in, eating nothing but apple cores, the empty pockets, empty pots, bread lines, picket signs, Lorca slumped on an Andalusian hillside—all that is years away. This is a moment. A tea pot is steaming, the old woman is putting a lid on the tin can—her face? It is turned away.

her face it is turned away

A sliver of a Muslim moon in the night sky and the smell of sausage in the air. Nothing will betray me, not the shape of my hands, nor the cold weather which greets my face as I walk out of the house, not the newspaper I buy with its propaganda, its political commentary, its sports scores, the old men at the pizza place talking for hours about the latest college game, the young couple leaning into each other's lives the way two trees lean into each other when there is a gentle breeze. Nothing will betray me today, not hot water or toilet fixtures, not three thousand feet of ash nor a film of snow from some Himalayan mountain, not rag weed or obsidian summer nights when the stars are bright bits of glass, not my two old shoes which carry me over the sidewalk, nor the sidewalk itself, cracked with the last lactuca pushing up towards the light, not the store fronts, the Spanish restaurant or the yuppified Doctoral students chewing down on tubule, the bars with their cracked light spilling sawdust the conversational tangents of drunks, not the frantic phone calls which lovers are making tonight, nor the neutral presence of strangers at bus stops, not the woman I pass on her porch with a blue shawl slung over her shoulders who waves, not her daughter jumping rope on the lawn, counting out songs in the late summer dusk, not the children who've opened the fire hydrant, not the old cars who can't start, their rust, the gentle swaying of someone's curtain they've just pulled and they turn on a light, I watch their silhouette walking carrying something, some meal that they spent hours making, how they will gather around the table, how I wish to them a goodnight.

a goodnight

Bus Station in Toledo, young woman with long braids, tied dyed shirt, balancing two children on either knee, the sound of the announcer's voice fading my eyes into sleep, conversation over my shoulder, two deep Southern women drawling about Al Green's latest Gospel show, just going through town, on their way to Gary Indiana, far as I can tell a homecoming of sorts, long time to come home, long time gone, the silver ships pulling up in clouds of steam, men bent over coffee at the counter— this is going I am dreaming, this is going fast, fading into cliche like trains, this Northern continent fading into rust, the glass factories gone, the parts plants, my friend Matthew's brothers would come stumbling home drunk, covered in grease, laugh at us glancing at their Hustler magazines, blasting Queen, George Clinton, Marvin Gaye, long gone as I write this, I miss my friend, last saw him in 86 washing dishes when I visited, Toledo, where I learned to play ball, far from my Brooklyn stoop, ran in the alleys, white kids and black, big afros and baseballs, Carolynn shaking her groove thing through seventy nine, no nostalgia, just the shiny wax of Michael's new Lincoln Continental, union man who pitched for us when we played ball, no Spike Lee before crack nostalgia wax, just young summers, broken bats, busted teeth, stealing hubcaps and wheeling them down the Junior High School halls.

Angels of anxiety, Eros, I am always running from my fear, of
unemployment, my elbow leaning into the wall, my son asleep
in his bed, he is sick, coughing, coughing, a cough is the
sound of an egg cracking Prevert wrote is a horrible sound,
the sound of hunger, Vallejo knew each bite of bread was a
piece taken out of another human being's mouth—this is
the consistency, I pass the schoolyard with its spikenards of
the social block, the boy by the chainlink fence no one has
asked to play, he is holding his hands behind his back, lean-
ing on one leg effeminately, he could die of his aloneness but
he will not, he will go on into the day as we all must go,
Camus, who knew to be a man was much harder than to be
a Saint, to embrace the world, to fight, the Saint disappears
into one's sorrow— praise the suffering, praise the poor, the
hungry, the alone, these are the people be damned, Patchen
who ranted at a time of war, *I hate the poor out of my love for
them* he wrote *Until all men unite in hating the poor, there can
be no new society. Stalin loves the poor—without them he could
not exist.* Against Seraphim. Saint Peter forgiven. *The poor
have been the slop pails of Capitalism, repositories for all the
filth and brutality of a filthy brutal world* The angel is weary. *I
say that property is murder.* The hands of dying children reach
upwards through your bread. Roads leading nowhere, where
Rilke? How must it stop? What Nomos? The glasses from
overfilling. Stop. To stumble the last steps up the church,
breaking the bread, the living raise their ready hands, O fa-
ther, in hell there is no fire, the Dervish who needed a light
snuck into hell in search of some fire and Eblise told him, we
have none, all men who come here bring their own, out on
the sidewalk in cold weather there is the sound of a sledge-
hammer, without fault you fought weeping, suddenly there

...17

are sirens, the old house remembers the fire-escape a deaf girl is signing, her sister humming *Killing Me Softly* offkey, she is lovely as tired eyes of the secretary, who is memorizing starcharts for the fireflies who bless the parks' trees, the strangers who wait for the trains, the bus, downtown, so many old ones I watch who sip their coffee, sneeze, the diners are full of the alone, hope without proper names, in rest stops the Preachers claim the apocalypse gathers through strangers, Lorca embraces his mentor, the Angels of Eros, in praise against them the Christians kneel and pray, the men who kneel without hope to lift boxes in the brute light of noon, the telephone won't ring in the warehouses, separated by aluminum siding, silence is freedom to Our fathers who art in heaven, the priests are forgiven, freedom is a cage, in the classrooms the teachers are calling for silence, the day has begun, the swing shift a few short years away, the sunlight is deep as their mother's arms, the children are dreaming of running through long grass like a skirt rising around them, *Is it surprising that prisons resemble factories, schools, barracks, hospitals, which all resemble prisons?*

prisons

Dogs barking, this oppressive world we must re-read, the Fifth graders they hand me their poems, brown children whose English teachers have silenced the Trinity of Spanish, English, & Lebanese—this classroom where I have said so little, this classroom how the children have dissolved its walls and invited in the light which falls in brilliant ladders across the floor, I asked them to write about their blocks, none chose to leave their apartments. They all read about their rooms, hallways, dolls, their grandmothers cooking, their brothers and sisters. They are *metaphysicians of the intimate*—all except one little boy whose *blue house is flying* but he doesn't tell us where it is going until a girl asks him and he says smiling, *He's taking me to you.*

he's taking me to you

Not Argentina or Antwerp, here in my hands. I am changing my son's diaper, he is learning to be toilet trained. He loves to sit on the plastic toilet, but he will not go. I watch myself frightened with him sometimes because is this self old and kind, translated the baby is now a child, blooming wept in the public schools, wept in the very last row. A man touches his wife, later a horse in full gallop. Silent, the huge crows gather on the power lines. My son scratches his head as we walk through the snow. Occasionally murderers encase their victims in snow. The couple we do not know will have triplets, down the long hospital hall one will let go, a nurse will cradle her in a blanket out of the room. My son will remember none of this. The crows gather, their wings are the black sails of Phoenician Death ships, their silhouettes are the billowing sheets of the social body, hushed day and night, *normalized...docile and capable*, shuddering. Can you hear my son crying? His feet are cold. He needs a new pair of shoes.

a new pair of shoes

Ideology, some History, the white man's bones, beliefs, brethren, the buffalo buried, the pyramids, to begin, the basalt, the bombs...you eyes like smoke, when I was eight years old, we walked out into the cold, saying these are my sisters, a certain blunder for the Baroque, the brilliant light of euphoric Nihilism, Nihilismus, *Dada Nihilismus,* Jones, the blues gone back and forth to the dark heart brother of the "low riders" there was a voice that spoke, turned your back beyond Blackness, past the Maskness toward the work inscribed in the struggle between classes, let there be Hurricanes unleashed, the radio speaks *the champion of the world,* nothing but nostalgia for a life sold...but you see Lenin the night feels heavy with your love of the factory, Lenin you never worked the night shift—those nights long ago I'd walk slow to the river, carrying you and old Leroi Jones, new Baraka, whispering a few words on the wet grass, when the rain came like a messenger from God, I claimed the luminous moment, there in the cold, I let go your book into the river, the long dark, dumbfounded, so long.

I am standing in the rain at the bus stop, my son is in daycare, the kids down the block are playing a game with a stick, *chi chi chi chi chi* go their tongues rattling off machine gun fire, until their mother appears on the porch and screams. I have seen the toy guns disappear from the neighborhood household's since the shootings. No blue florescent Lugars, or super soakers, no plastic sawed off shotguns or three barreled super Star Wars wet dream automatic icons of the insane. The mothers have smashed them & left them on the sidewalk: Bits of colored plastic scattered when the garbage truck comes to carry them away in the cold rain.

in the cold rain

Where was I? On the block outside the state prison in Auburn, New York on the last night of the State Fair, we drove the wrong way, ended up at Connie's Tex Mex where the Black women, the Latin women, the poor white women, up from the city, the small farms, sat after their visits, talking, showing pictures, how one sister sighed *how long since last time your man was released, feels like we've been sitting here for decades.*

for decades

To be found alone on a strange street, to be found with empty
pockets and no ID, to be found asleep on the train with no
money, to be found in shiny shoes on a Saturday night by a
slim woman, a sun washed mural Billy's voice waiting through
a long traffic light, to be found in an empty parking lot, a
burial ground, a rhapsodic sound of hard candy and just
washed clothes on the crowded dance-floor that fragrance
like tropical rain and all the comforts of home, to be found in
the last cigarette smoked after working the second shift, and
you close your eyes because jazz is a theory that singes loan
payments into ash, to be found in the bar when Judas is
buying the rounds with Saint Michael and Joan of Arc is
kicking someone's ass in the back, to be found in a Country
and Western song when "everything in your life seems wrong,"
to be found by your father, by your mother, to be found on
the ground holding your head by the guard, to be found by
the streetlight, by the deaconess praising the light by the body
by the trembling web to be found in the snow, old and alone
without kids, working the night shift at the Citgo station, to
be found so elegant the last streetcar backs up to pick you up,
to be found asleep with the wrong answer, to be found under
the nun's ruler, to be found unemployed, underground, un-
sound, underpaid, underpressure is not to be found hallelu-
jahs, and crazy shit like real cools, and *to leap from a ledge of
language* into the crowd, to be found, to be found Luckless
with Lucille with a five dollar bottle of brandy and a pack of
Luckies in the backseat of your mama's car, to be found un-
shaven and shrunken, to be found tremendously boogie back-
stage, to be found freedom, to be found feeling too old to be
found, to be turning translucent in the fifth floor light of
thorazine to be 'Trane worshipped swiveling in the wake of

this indigo silk dress to be found Cinderella on a back alley spring night surrounded by switch blades to be found blinded by the vestments of a just life rising at dusk, to be found burned by Rachel's grief, to be found ironing your sink washed shirt in New Orleans behind the iron fusillade of some cheap motel where you are forgetting your aching knee, your hangover, to be found staring at the sparrow settled outside the window is to be found worthwhile with wonder and with loss...spread your wings.

spread your wings

Back on the downtown bus, I watch this man, his dirty face the color of Russian Christ. He wore a woolen hat pulled down over his ears and a long Parka and was carrying a small green Gideon Bible he placed on the seat beside him. He took off his right shoe (I noticed he didn't have socks on) and began to rub his unusually swollen foot. He turned to me and said, *If I start to speak to myself it's because when I ask myself sometimes I hear God is suffering.*

God is suffering

I was dreaming I had a word folded into me...the unadorned simplicity inside a hospital room, changing my socks on the edge of a bed, I could barely take food—they'd never let loose a laugh sometimes no matter the theory, was it so long ago, *the basic recipe for the reification of institutions is to bestow on them an ontological status independent of human activity and signification:* the faces behind the glass, the pullers of levers, the dispensers of pills, Paxil, Ritalin, dis-identification I shrink to the vanishing point—if you don't look over your shoulder you can't tell who you've been.

My neighbor Michael's smoking a joint out on his porch, 9:43 AM, white cup on the railing, shadows pool inside the hall, like March weather or withered trees we can see the ruins—unraveling I say to myself, the drunken episodes longer, the children are riding their bikes around the corner, pink tassels sway from A—'s handlebars (she laughs), I notice Michael is swaying in place, his eyes are closed, wings are sprouting from his shoulders, he is falling somewhere which claims him (in the news they've found a Spanish galleon), say have you seen the way a man walks from a bar in daylight to be startled by children playing, what is it to confound The House of Heaven, the worried Gods, (like when I was five the empty hive we found in my friend's attic, he blew his breath across it like a Pan flute)— try to remember when bird's panic, like once you're dead, avoid saying the word "husk," it is there before the tulips push through the ground, you resolve to watch the days a certain saint a single mother washing her child's hands, working the night shift (a motel clerk) drawing a map in the margins, or are you grading children's texts, whose back has bent into a chair, what is the shape of sorrow, what desk holds it in place, you walking you clutching a handful of change (will anyone) you who wear my father's face (unbelievably sweet), for a long time the spine pangs, I hear a banging from someone's kitchen across the garage, there were sirens as I slept, the drive away the radio claims the volume tuned to tremble, someone's coffin a stranger carried, Sunday itself resigns, after a long Saturday night my shirt is seeped with cigarette smoke and I wake to hear the Bible women rehearse the walk past Saint Peters in their long dresses on their way to church across the street they are clutching their scriptures, they are discussing the

weather I recognize in their faces the fragrance of azaleas —
from a tall dark woman a Georgia accent drawls unsettling
the sequence of bare branches full as the hat on her hair, she
tugs at her small daughter, vibrant as a whistle, up the stone
steps, they disappear into the church—drawn to the wine
inside the heart starts to shudder and begins to sing, the con-
gregation shaking the rafters, Michael closes his eyes, hum-
ming along, I watch him sway (I am filling with his music) as
if filling with a music I almost think he believes.

The SUNOCO sign another sad evening, the light plays over the hills, could it be that even God hiding inside those bulbs the intimate life achieved in small moments the words I recite: Daydreams, wounds, interruptions, walls leaning toward the shape of trees, illness meaning a great lie, Leviathan of Genre, merely "political," the Romantic Era of *humanism,* floats one if further proof, a passing window—how much for the word in miniature, vocal chords to shake that Latin three stories down into a snow globe city: in one hand a tomb, in the other a hummingbird's nest: two hands, hold them both behind your back then open your fists, an old parlor trick, to extend speech with its hard adherence to refract like Monk's riff leaving the room because the eye not the sky conceives the thesis of its images: *justified by the fact that nothing is so completely at variance with human nature as this*...of course, Freud meant *to love one's neighbor as oneself*...but what about that SUNOCO sign melting as a *thing* until 3:00 A.M. much less than ordinary when I drive by on my way to get aspirin & my eyes reflect *it* for all dreamers of forms the geometric stillness in the lived the human psyche to make us listen through the absolute evening at a long traffic light prodding us with primitive houses I leave through the door I came in.

30...

Downtown Syracuse, what can be wrong? This tall woman crying among the oranges at the open air market, the spaces between the stalls are filling with the sound of her voice, she is in her fifties, she has a yellow scarf around black hair, dark striking Italian eyes, she is weeping into her hands, throwing her head back, she is standing in front of a shopping cart full of just bought vegetables, bread, cheese, which tells me she is not crazy— something has happened, it is as if the woman in front of her holding the bag of fruit has just told her that someone they both knew is dead.

Crates of onions and my great-grand-father's soda bottle factory, industrial lords and petty contractors, in the motionless light the names written out the tedium of years, which would sanction a jail for differences for the underground now must find another face, nerves of lead bleed the radio in parentheses, a theory of a broom the earth could use and at 11:PM, after a short barrage the ambiguities of Lana Tuner re-emerge in the Art House's on-coming lights, laughter, these blues notes I write in the social night before I rise to teach in the schools, here in this theater I search for some of the same faces, there are all the addicts with their heads swung back, the college students' little giggles and pretentious talk, to think and fuck with rippling muscles and the wonderful clouds and the role of the revolution is to be young, the attempt to find Rouen cathedrals in your lover's eyes, the hustlers call a sincerity I could trust in the jesters' gestures, the screen fades and they are out talking in the bitter bars, the heart-break and breath of a busy age, there are frantic blondes and slight Phillippino boys with brash eyeliner, and I am pondering the cost of a statue's hips in a store window, the amusement of lips, the cool night, a grope of dejected ballads that the wind works between walking slightly ebullient in the rain because it's the benighted El Nino I find the meaning as long as the limbs so many more than in the Victorian fields, these streets which sigh the human world as feeling ever thinner *The little animal fights back* so to speak stunned by the oncoming headlights I recall that whole car mural I saw earlier in the evening painted by some brash boy with a backwards baseball cap, unsung Diego Rivera from The Bronx, riding the trains of paint over the Island to Spanish Harlem, those shimmering lights, those hours between Michaelangelo and Basquiat, be-

tween Brahms and Boogie Down, the ground shakes before
the silence of people passing, persuades you not to ask their
names, we forget each other's faces like the strange face on a
two dollar bill that flew from the book of a linguistics profes-
sor (I asked him after) sitting between the twin stone lions in
front of the 42nd Street Library—his white Einsteinian hair
wild as I bend to catch his bill he is shouting, "It's the first
one ever printed," waving a copy of The Secrets of Sanskrit,
laughing nervously into my face as if he is afraid I won't hand
it back, "I use it as a bookmark," he explains.

he explains

In the dark all night, Friday late breathing you lean, the holy
names, neither of us mean, like Jesus and not knowing, the
first time, I had been sweeping, a human voice...of sad...which
are mingled *con el vino*, the old autumn, the snow is coming
I tell my son, he is leaning over to see the sky, the drowned
woman is grieving up there, I am dreaming, in the holy milk
with a girl I saw pickup trucks—the salesman said he drives
a new model, the original prize, in Italy so many we met
thought all Americans were given new cars at sixteen, had
shiny suburban houses, those street kids playing soccer by
the Ufizzi, how they couldn't believe I worked in a factory,
had saved for three years for that trip, how they couldn't hear
my accent (class), the years biting inwards, the hardened body
of bread, they were tall weeds running through the
cobblestoned streets, you must know my heart was in them.

them

I notice the leavings outside the bars, the lounge of the mental homes, the methadone stops, there is no getting up how can you now the rain comes in from the river, so much caressing, and all the young queens who make demands said of the current state of corners, *They'll just pick you up,* these plainclothed detectives, harassing teenagers wearing dresses, wigs, in New Jersey today that breath the breeze rustles I am guarding it from the cops, the sounds of the street, three hours until a train home, and the wind dies down to nothing except ordinary speech, the unserious and unceasing chit chat we seldom hear, for these of an afternoon it is sweet and I am unable to unlisten and so find this talk, and this white kid is thin and effeminate and alone he is counting the days to himself, in his pocket (I hope) is a prescription I cannot see, there are calm somethings that assume the world echoes loneliness but also there no less disfiguring, jailed with the waiting and despair he says *Here I am, a person,* an undefined tenderness in a remote cloister I notice how the light cannot but trace his face transformed into torch songs he hums to the train's departure, relaxed now as he counts backwards towards the deepening un-certainty of someone, perhaps your, embrace.

perhaps your embrace

Children in cancer wards. They are metaphysicians of the simple, who will know us, they ask? Under the El a river of lotus blossoms. Farewell. Every room is flooded for many birds bring the children ribbons. Children in the middle with the dead face she jabs, a hug comes. I mean it. No, your mother wailing with rage. Who will know us? For what's not is ours. In faces. There is no doubt. The innocent first question worshipped. Another name for milk. Kin. A miraculous alchemy.

Farewell.

Louie has been arrested. I hear the cops talking at the corner store. They found him half naked in someone's doorway complaining about ants on his skin. The children for the first time in weeks are silent. It is as if they are waiting outside a prison. There are at least twelve of them sitting around his bench. Autumn is nearing its end.

A sparrow on the ledge of a Brooklyn Apartment. Braque's quivering leap, Cubist wings. Children who will tell the hush? That will ultimately transform the incomprehensible...

Children cold, at lunch you mustn't forget the sound of car tires, the shortcut to your grandmother's lap. Children crisscross the world to a snowscape from heaven, whistles, Einstein's brain, silk pajamas, in every corner of the sofa there are continents mapped.

Synagogues that fill the air.

Children will you always love me? Will you shake down the Second Coming? Attracted to small change and far away places. Children bring me a gift from the sea so I may wander where I've been. Children the Devil is hiding in the highest beam of the house. He is wearing the face of the shoe shine boy. He is smiling. Do not listen to that gibberish. The Gypsy's do not worship Saint Anthony. Only Sausage makers. Auto shop patrons scanning used magazines, distraught. Children I offer you a quarter for the gumball machine. Children beware of the kitchen drawer. Your father has turned on the stove. Go outside, flying in the sky there are a dozen cranes and a blue guitar.

Children down the long stairs must it be believed that Johnny Mathis still matters? Children without an encore, without heroes, asking for the journey to end. Children with a terminal disease, some song modern and expansive at 5:AM there is a doll's head on the street. Evidence of the unjust. But there is gospel in a cornflower pushing up through the sidewalk. Ballerinas of the imagination, the children become weightless with everything they love. They turn snowdrifts tender with their angelic arms. Children expel halos in the cold wind when they run. They become steam engines, little trains, they are closer than the woman sobbing in the room above you. There are inside her, if you listen they are inside you. Children leaving wind-chimes in the winter sun.

Children beware the difficult. The poor moon is the most simple of shapes. Niagara Falls we must worship: a mother running a comb through her daughter's hair.

Children and winos. Cops. Good luck. *You want Culture?* Sunlight on the corner bench. Louie is sleeping. The children are planning their attack. The cops are telling the shop owner how this guy got difficult last night and they had to rough him up. It is seventy degrees in November, almost flagrant the wind will turn freezing over night. I will go to bed drunk, dream I can't raise my eyelids, that it is summer and I am hearing children singing nursery rhymes while I am sleeping outside...

Children of pop bottles collected for nickels, of bath water and blue sailboats. Children have become aware of certain things. In the dark, do you remember? Children shaking their heads over their grandmothers' visions of saints, urging them that winos are perverts, deviants, drunks. Their fathers left out of the equation. Algebra for the innocent to decipher. *Cipher.* Little *shits.* Mr. Potatohead is dead. Cellophane flames. Gone the good kick of a crushed can. Across the fields of the street they come trudging through the snow, children sharp as farm implements. Early in the AM, before the sun has risen, they are waiting for the school bus. They are huddled. One begins to move. Then another. Toward another.

They are just beginning to learn how to dance.

to learn how to dance

My neighbor Ray's kind of crazy (in that way so many of us are) he keep's a gun in the closet ("just in case") he sits on the porch all evening till dark (drinking Milwaukee's best and smoking cigarettes) somewhere along the way he keeps his grass mowed and his trees trimmed (but I never see him work on it) he knows everything there is to know about cars (he works as a mechanic, quits his jobs, gets another), he keeps a spit shined 73 Cadillac coup de Ville under a blue tarp in his backyard (my dream car, the kids in the avenue call it Old School), he "cares about the neighborhood", the kids—he's a white man who's watched some of the black kids grow to fall into "dumb trouble," (as he puts it) he watches out for some of them; they come and sit on the porch with him (like everyone else in the neighborhood), he tells them stories about "fixing things," about "fast cars," they talk and talk and talk and when needed he gives advice—I overhear LaShon (fifteen years old) tell his girlfriend, "yeah, he's like my father—except, of course, he's white."

Dubois and destiny, destinudo, nude, the man on the auc-
tion block, wood, would 'one lie breed a hundred' thousands,
Dubois past eighty still talking about his Encyclopedia
Africana, before he died, black consciousness was auctioned,
to let the bones dictate is to be dead, or to deny, find authen-
tic jukeboxes in dives, but drop a quarter and you'll still hear
corporate schemes for grinding indigenous beats into hid-
eous hits, these shapes I shift open eyed, let the subject which
restricts the lived know whose pain ceased gripping, only
hemlocked Socrates is smoked by the flash fire choked His-
tories, there's a bit of Ghandi dropped, one certainty there is
no remembrance of former things like the man said who sold
it this refusal with fight is enormous in the street the speaker
called Being and art are as closely bound on a page about to
become, begun unraveling the form like a fine sweat, remind-
ing us the *difereance',* a world of things so lovely somewhere
between childhood and addiction I thought I was working
the entire orchestra of winter, a kind of laughter let loose, a
kind of thing-*ing* with radiance, what kept going a kind of
labor, a kind of lilt, not *the human condition in the political
tradition of prior thought,* but action itself only upon making
violence a form of *un*making, a sphere of *un*making, a form
of sad occupation the tossed salt shimmers in the moon light
on the warehouse floor, picking their noses there is a light
inside those on the loading dock, long ago I stood with these
built men, black, white, one speaking Spanish, he pauses to
spark a Cuban cigar, that city of shadows, of old stories lit
with the living, a kind of tent these enclosed lives, despite
the invisible...to drive home into newsprint, instead eat the
hard bread, the solitary language of two bodies nobody hears
in this darkness colliding who knows one's voice, the parent

cradling the child, this who can resist, to the booted ones swollen half shut all women are wounds, can you hear them make explicit their points, conscripted—but what if the wind of the rooms, the bondage of noon and night, a suitcoat without any money, a house that needs paint, the child asleep on the stairwell, what if what I have unfolds to describe the coming as the leaves to a tree, this singing that inhabits the night must open who is indistinct, to gain a living and blessedness against illness is indeed what follows the line of children singing, speech that's too deep is a landscape of Hoodoo along the oiled avenues of everything off, there I am reading a comic book on the bus as a child, give me lemons for lemonade on a yellow table cloth, give me rag men and redbones, give me a hurdy-gurdy to play for the blind man and his hot lapping dog, the window is down and the wind is winding the world like a music box, the chiming of freeze tag and toy cars, the cops at the corner by the corner store, give me a portable john, a bad garage band, a signifying snake criss-crossed with Coltrane and Saint Van Gogh, give me *guaguaco* and Kyoto's white gardens, graveyards of old Anarchists outside of Barcelona, where the dead rest their heads, give them drums so they may find their way home to that neighborhood without meaning beyond Buddha's lap where the baby Jesus is napping, where the Celtic princesses are raising their swords against the Roman hordes, give me plum prints and laughter of my son's eyes, a circle of girls in the schoolyard sharing a cigarette, give me Satchel Paige's wind-up and Che Guevera's last smoke, for the earthquake is almost upon us the Preacher is crying at the Baptist Church on the corner, his words are all broken class, give me a language that includes all life and I will lift it up blindly calling across waters the thousand daughters to rise for what moves us is what happens when sadness is too sweet for the jukeboxes to shimmy notes through the dancehalls of ghosts...They're here tonight at this dance, all the gone faces, the worried attached to the unfamiliar, the jaded and the beginner, the justified and the forgiven, here they will mingle until all tones give over, dwarfed down to the last letter— was it only yesterday when our voices gathered our ancestors, the endless bargaining, was it too much to ask, to come home to, and love these scraps is to love the human inscription, that step upwards a document I uphold as a step against the parts of you that lie, as when a hill fills half the sky, to re-find a dream-womb while dreaming, to re-play in your mind a film reel of this hallow life, in reverse, while leaving.

in reverse while leaving

What stood defined, on a slope of sunlight, with clarity to be awakened running, you won't find bread and wine in the fields, but no one is working this sunrise, instead they are searching, this early when even the children are still asleep, they are climbing through the birches, the dogs barking, they are following their breath through this stillness, they are longing, they are calling out witness against the trees.

Like the long ladder of *A Love Supreme*, the inevitability of
meaning: ain't it great your city so very interesting, your city
of coats and scarves, pupils and saints, dancers arching to the
clatter of pool halls, your city of fluttering verbs, of blue urges
and laments like the rain that can cure insomnia, read halos
like diamonds of whiskey tossed down the mine of a throat,
city of the beautiful signboards, convexed as a thought, curved
as your gaze on the train, or the forms of Phillip Guston, this
city of claustrophobia and free speech (which is free forms or
free cheap like chains) which means this consumer junk, the
market stalls, the street vendors blankets of trinkets, illegal
imports into the geometry of avenues that are always *occupado*,
city of being social, of hunger, of coughs and sonatas that
inscribe the trembling drum of loudspeakers, embarrassingly
clear, your breath groups Bop, as if subtlety fascistic brokers
break out into *Summertime* on the subway platform, this city
of bridges and beats that all the world's ills scream themselves
out in the currency of swanky stores and white shirted ad-
dicts entering high office buildings, the great length between
the unopened door of the Statue of Liberty and the El rising
beyond the tenement's skyline like the lines of the page we
write letters on as a child, forget the seventh level of hell
begins on a street corner, so does the choreography of a dance,
see the pretty ones waltzing with Dante over there in Hell's
Kitchen, Catacombs of ears down at the infirmary the doc-
tors as secretly splicing genes, the Gnostics are selling the
cross on Seventh Avenue where I am five years old running
away from the Oklahoma of my grandmother, her tongue
talks to crows and grows roses, my grandfather there on the
Lower East Side sharing a cigarette with a gang of Puerto
Rican kids, they want to play pool, not one has gone to school

today, they are exchanging the revolution for the forgetting haze of a needle's eye, my mother is down at the welfare office, and Yonkers is filled with the relatives I have never seen— my gentile grandmother betrothed to a Moldavian Jew was enough to bar all windows, send synagogues shivering that is to forget here in this city of my childhood, the Good Humor Man is still playing his tune, the architecture of the east river still rising into view, and what does this tell you about the present there it is brothers, are all solutions made of fragments, the system shudders, sunlight, this endlessly non-existent aching which has become the ruins and the beautiful and the blues.

Suddenly there is Robert Desnos tangoing with the daugh-
ters of the disappeared in an Argentine bar, as in Suarez's
film, sitting there is Jesus or the idea of Him hidden in the
graceful limbs of thin men, drugged with the partisans, in
prisons, executioners, in itself by luck all the beautiful
bleedings, when a decision forms as if the whole sky opens as
if the dead birds of extinct species lift their wings...in the
light of a bare light bulb a man is sharpening a razor, this is
terrible, like a theatre, the way what happened, can't be re-
called, the forgetting of such simple things, the opposite of
Cocteau, the architecture of dreams...Sundiata rushing
Memen horseman across the Sudanese sand...sometimes there
is a holy light I used to argue in not-remembrance...a sad
cafe named Frank Stanford, two shots to the sweetheart's ear,
there is a gigolo on the horizon, a staircase of shoes, here in
my body, in my two hands, I am attempting to hold the air,
to interpret these thoughts no one has heard of ever since I
gave up Miles for dinner, I turned him back into *Kind of
Blue*, closed my eyes and flew out the window of my closed
lids to find goldfish feeding beneath a rippling Japanese moon,
to run incognito through fields of poppies in Thailand, run
through North American cities where fire hydrants drain the
summers into streets where tourists never tread, to under-
stand the ill light of witnessing, what's wrong here is *I never
compared my love* to the simple things (Stanford), the hours:
hands of the clock, how slow they move, and there are those
Neruda odes, simple as giant turtles rising to breathe in the
great wind, or Death pushing for the deepest oar, and the
moon hung tethered on a high chord, there above the trees
where a body is swaying, my father is four in the fifties riding
with Anna on a southbound train, in the backwoods and

backyards the apartheid is unraveling into the abstract, *but hegemony falters,* which is why I *can* claim Dolphy as my mentor, he is just *this side* of the esoteric, where I belong, and there is Robert Desnos, there is Cocteau...come, walk with us down the long hallway of opening arms.

down the long hallway of opening arms

Let my neighbor Michael light incense every night and dance
naked in the attic with a flashlight so that his old limbs are
well-pleasing in his sight, as ants will dance on sugar, let my
neighbor bang pots and pans and let his children simmer in
the Buddisatvas disguises, let him affirm himself with the
stretch of his arms, let him breath a wind of poppies and TV
buttered popcorn, his large wife in her tie dyed sundress out
hanging the wash on the lawn, let him forget the overture of
his lack of courage and manage an illuminating preoccupa-
tion with the shape of her shoulders, as he sits smoking every
night on the porch let the *aura of toolshops* fill his head with
light as when his wife Leslie baked him a sweetcake and I saw
him swing her through the kitchen holding on to her huge
arms the way the wind will grab a hundred foot oak and rock
it before leaving it still … let him not raise his voice tonight
and throw his shoes at the kids who laugh at him because he
is too drunk to chase them, let there be answers to all their
questions, let his returnables not seek him relentlessly bal-
anced on a stool, let the crackling vinyl of his old Country
and Western forty-fives he plays on the plastic record player
become clean as Orphelias, let nouns like *Mudfaced* and *ma-
chinery* fill his tongue, as he picks up the old guitar I heard
him tell his wife he bought at a yard sale, and the family
pauses in disbelief, as he slowly, and gently, begins to strum.

to strum

Why blame me, my argument. Metaphor and displacement, Derrida: between two signs, one and the other. The Other: an opponent, or as Levinas says, *the face of God*: the lighted rain is still in the vastness where we walked already the men working, so quiet the little birds beside the abandoned shoes by the side of the road, and then the lean years came, the years of hunger, frozen, the snow, those Syracuse streets where I walked alone beneath streetlights, looking for justice, his beard, waving little farewells to my past, there are some dimes that should never be left as tips on the counter, bars where the patrons eyes are too familiar, buses where strangers join hands. There is the phenomenon of displacement, the causality of temporality, a theory to suggest sovereignty, metaphors for home, where the absence brings the presence, the body becomes into being, that cathedral of sorrows, fill it with your mama's sweet potato pies, suckle it with grace, deny the heft of the hammer, embrace the boy in a wheelchair, his twisted limbs, where is Dante to question God, lead us through the seventh level of suffering, those good unbaptised Christians and their "sighs," where is the angel Gabriel to lead Abraham to heaven, in the plush darkness where *even Yiddish becomes a tragic tongue* (Stern) the inner connection, society is a soil, name us folk-artists throwing up crumbs, we are awake with him, sweaty and stinking, the country between us to tell about beauty that comes apart, carousels of farewells, who can tell us the dust collects the dying, how many men this winter, for the sadness of my heavy head I make a bed of my hands.

Criminals and carnivals, late summer and the State Fair has closed down…forget Post-Structuralist theory, it won't help you un-stake a tent…the long line of trailers, horses, sheep, the night sky filled with the oinking of pigs…and the fairgrounds…forgettable, all the Anglo Saxon chronicles of debris … Chrysalis, of Clinical Depression remains while you move upwards or downwards on the stairs … Chernobyl is back in the news, the bursting bellies, Golden Pagodas of piglets, the Ukraine's black earth, the woman no older than me on the International Channel spreads her arms in that universal gesture of the helpless, the misshapen child in his wheelchair … amputate the limbs, the plastic hand of Ms. Mary our teacher's aid in elementary school, how it didn't quite match the brown of her skin, Ruel asked her, *Do they only got one shade for Black people?* Praise the pure poverty of keeping a straight face, praise the most everyday absentee-ism, abandoning work, and deception, praise deception the best, praise the articulation of anarchy in the language of leaves, praise the autonomy of the birds singing, praise the single solitary blessedness of any ordinary day, bless the aesthetics of stones and the tremulous hands of the old man whom the night sky loves as he lumbers through the night stand for aspirin telling Death to wait his turn and to go back in the kitchen and fry up some sausages, beware of Vegans who raise their lids … gas chambers and essentialists are surely related … into sleep the Pleiades are blessed the long streets of the word whereas to refrain from fighting for suffrage, the birth of the *housewife* forget us the cabin, no chopping wood abandoning work we sit alone afternoons but scars of a river, her body, her bones. And now some years she hears the children, the empty staircase, the lawn, they are closing the gates, the gas lights are gone, the gas stove is lit, *all this time I was dying, I didn't know my own skin.*

This then, of all this history, even amid despair, to some touches, that should reveal again and again an image sprung partly in dread: Bicultural. Bipolar. Buy a dozen donuts at the donut shops. Blaring neon. Cops. Muscular boys. For the sake of. Bus-stops. Beauty pageants. I can tell by the way she walks. Inscribed on the body. The site of its own destruction. Instructions: when a body takes a body for granted, the breath fills with gasoline, words...But to be unseen. Or seen? That waitress I watched in Detroit in Greektown, the way she leaned against the doorway for a moment, ran a hand through her damp hair...That *gesture.* I *took.* Or walking home from school as a child the older Black kids would punch me in the head. I counted bruises, learned to duck swift, run. Someone whiter might've burned into a bad theory. But I grew six inches one summer, swung fast, it didn't matter who bit. I had a match between my teeth, the schoolyard all broken glass and busted noses, long before I read Ghandi I breathed swish as the silent towns faded from the yellow bus, driving from gym to gym in junior high, I lit up for over twenty ten games in a row, once overheard an opposing coach exclaim*, I never seen a white kid push the ball so fast*...So to apologize for survival, or else a state of mind, already there is a rhythm *sister been seen running across the marketplace,* from *Sundiata* I sing for my cousin Danny was named *yellow* as a child, the other children teased her into a kaleidoscope of invisible scars, later in life I search for the incisions in her flesh, she is becoming a form of forgetting, the buried notes waving goodbye when she backs out the door without a coat, the wind outside is cold, she has sidestepped the dread of being fired, this dialogue with the dead, the dust collects on her childhood, into the syringe of the female body, viewed through the colonial lens, infiltrating the inarticulate tongues, a system defined from inside, occupied...she has dark circles under her eyes, sometimes she disappears for days.

For some things everything depends, if you want to see what's new in near perfect conditions for witnessing the art of witnessing, for some things allow us to leave, but how do you contain your hurt when of him or her you can not stop thinking, how Dalton was murdered for inscribing letters by hand. She tried to explain this you tell me, but you *were young and stupid back then*. To be bourgeois is to prefer to believe you are good, so what does that say when the underpaid workers arrive for the nightshift at 9:30 PM, you claim their bodies the opposite *of even a section of those who were almost*...the danger of theory is to reduce a human being to a text...*signify your own fucked up white life* someone once cried in a graduate class...outside of the church of whose own hands what can one know...the opposite of parasols on a bright promenade, far from the concept of masses, far from the saving of medieval laughter, the sunlight tilts the women's hats and all of France at the century's dramatic close...the color of Victorian lace replaced with the garish gasmask (fetish), sunlight "dappled" across a pool "dappled" is a word of denial, even the dead are turning their heads in the sand, on the hillsides *das fallen,* the fallen *I shall call everyday people* and the avant-garde drunk on too-much tangential junk, in the night-time the hillsides are filled with flickering lights like *the dying of fireflies*, the long rows of miners at the edges are pressing their thumbs and forefingers over the candles on their heads, who has written of the catacombs beneath The City of Lights, a *doorway for deviants, everything non-white*, (out of the Metro tunnel a slender Algerian boy climbs onto the platform, calls out in Berber to no one I can see, runs through a door) a decade or so before the assembly lines of Detroit opened wide, the strikers how many died, Italian fascists sighed with their love of El Duce's eloquent hands, all those magnificent manifestos in French, forgive me a figurative or two, one strangle or another how far Ezra slides from "I pay men to talk of peace," for some things depend upon another feature of living, verbal feats *don't mean no man no good* Surely this raging the ruling class emerged, *praise the white lies...who started these discussions...in days of yore...all bourgeois poetry is an expression of the bourgeois illusion* of Culture and Good there is little chance the resistance must extend because *I am we find it was not so for this* assaultment of power these words reduced reworked rewritten rewarned from where raged a riot let burn, did I mention Detroit earned all that rage against eight mile apartheid watching the pins fall on a Saturday night, my Orthodox friends father threw three strikes and *never let THEM into this neighborhood...everyone naturally inclines...to the rhythm...with thorns and thistles...*but nowhere near are the night when the left hand seeks Requiem seeks Requiem shrieks Requiem, Aida dies, let the veil fall from the kid in the attic who *puts on his mother's wedding dress,* Lorca was right, there are events that reveal the reverse, the hillsides are buried with them, when is the father a form of fear for some grounds distinguish our experience, a terrible patriarchal wind, or is it a prayer? Saturdays the Christians are boycotting *faggot businesses,* all the arcane knowledge let loose isn't witness, *guileless fools,* those magnificent seizings— and the sky is filled with crows, and my son is running in circles calling to them like his grandmother, in the park the young queer Korean woman is directing a movie, calling out in jagged English, to shoot *the close-up* of the human face, they focus on one eye, a woman staring back at the camera, suddenly pointing at you. For some things from city to city the unspeakably charmed, of the epoch concerned, an interesting sociological study. For some things tomorrow it will be cool, but cloudy and after some time it will grow dark and it will be impossible to see us do this for some things to say a simple example: *I love another, but cannot love myself...a critique born of reflection...on a familiar road....for a pool freely flowing*...for some things there are reverberations, re-verbs, nations, volumes of unopened books in the basements, boxes of bullets, hooks...for some things *dying will be easy*, say Amen, say *unselfishness...is the life of an old maid*...say *the human condition in general...distortion...unmolested by foreigners*...say to be human for some things *one can be white, colored, or black depending upon how white people classify you*...for some things are broken on the banks of the bad Mississippi, *the persistence of its lyrics,* the persistence of living, a persistence of broken strings, a sort of almost silenced song meaning for some things there is a music beyond even music, beyond even musing, for some things sing without saying so, as when the city bus heaves and my tiny son laughs and throws his hands in the air, as when he danced in a circle the first day it snowed.

Apparitions, appearances, my son pointing at something in the corner of the room, there by the ceiling, I should know better but there is apprehension, the gas heat grumbles through the walls and I think somehow here, the holy Virgin descending. Don't laugh. There is background: The old madres are chanting the rosary again, I can hear them through the floor. I could tell you a story for there are instructions for seeing the world is not as mysterious as what our strength claims, the time of leaving cannot be said the languages that are known house gleaming words when my son stands up he points *there*, and I shudder before I realize the flickering's from a passing car's headlights...But months ago I wondered how to quiet without waking this woman, snoring there on the AMTRAK she was forty or so falling into the seat across from me, I could hear the pop songs pleading through her headphones, and I was dreaming of the rain turning to salt as I pulled into a station, outside of Cleveland, to touch the lip of sorrow, the city escapes becomes a ship suddenly there on the shore of some sure realism I had such a vision of form against the failure of remembrance in the loose black blouse of the Hassidic woman walking down the isle, how considerate her eyes and the small boy she pulled behind her, the father with his tall hat and black shoes, minor shadows, strangers, there as if what was called came into view, I rubbed my eyes, sighing, outside the stained window was a view of winter, smokestacks, factories where men bent half hell'd over the machines, whatever time it was is over, bird's feet in the eyes of the man who asked the porter where he could get a drink of water this human telling should say nothing without meaning a sort of singing, even the winter's translucent grayness through the stained window (I thought of bombed out cathedrals), like Pasternak, that scene with the horsemen on the steppes, this passing large spaces, the woman across from me awakened, staring out the window she stretched yawning as if rejoicing...and strangely I saw my grandfather starting to sob as he told me of riding the haycart to Prague as a child, how he loved to glance down and watch the horse's great hooves clodding through the clay.

clodding through the clay

Certain politicians would have made good Aztecs, their love
of sacrifices to the sun (Son), certain politicians have dreams
of the Roman coliseum, they sit in the senate seat and raise
the baton (see the women mobilizing in front of the clinic,
the good cross carrying Christians) the assumptions in the
shadows, a brutal precondition, the bus passes by, someone
shouts *gun,* see certain politicians do not want to make vis-
ible the unseen, they see what they say makes it so, a re-
telling of the story, historically speaking *women are given lim-
ited agency,* dying of whiteness this heavy moment fills the
air, a sudden falling gesturing at all the windows—children
in yellow raincoats skipping through puddles, mother cover
their eyes from placards, certain politicians cannot ascertain
dead women, they ascertain the boy with the gun is simply
bad, certain politicians haunt my father's dreams, tap him on
the shoulder and smile, a form of disease, paranoia the doc-
tors would inscribe, *inscribe* is a form of technological inci-
sion, like the intersection of the literary and the
historical(Loomba)—not surprisingly an individual enters
ways of ordering culture, Molotov cocktails that flame in C
sharp, as when zootsuited crazy shit inscribes a new line in
the book of inspirations' errors, this is serious trouble certain
politicians mandate life for what was misdemeanors, the pro-
noun *they* is inscribed, hide behind the gated communities,
to commute is a political event, to forget that *they* and *we*
and *I* are overlaid, the dismantling of this then is what *they*
would not be telling you—I watched those Southern Bap-
tists marching through the rough outline of biographies and
laments that cling to the cables of the continental divide, all
those ancient lies that still play in twenty first century ser-
mons, but this soliloquy is but a little song that claims we

hesitate when everywhere the barren trees are ghosts you can breathe.

Among victims is to be everywhere at millennium's end, ex-
humed and lifted, message bringer, the rhythm such that
Lamentation seems like a stand-up comedy routine. But speak-
ing the universe enters a church, out of a desolate place into
an asylum, and everyone I love digs into this earth to find a
doorway to walk through...to re-find our everyday words, we
must recall The Fall, the failure, fraught, must replace it with
a summer evening, a city's opened fire hydrant, the neigh-
borhood children splashing in the dark, till they become the
dark itself, those not so distant voices which overwhelm—

Notes

P. 9 "If they father...," from the Biblical parable; "Could I kill ..." medieval mystic Henry Suso.

P. 13 Irish Nationalist Charles Steward Parnell. The Belgium Congo refers to the genocidal slave labor policies of King Leopold .

P. 14 Pepe is my wife Suzanne Proulx's grandfather; he was a French Canadian mill worker.

P. 17 French surrealist poet Jacques Prevert; Peruvian surrealist poet Caesar Vallejo. Some of the italicized lines are from Kenneth Patchen's *The Journal of Albion Moonlight*.

P. 17 The last lines of the poem are from Michele Foucault's *Discipline and Punishment*.

P. 21 *Dada Nihilismus* is a book of poems by Leroi Jones

P. 40 The Encyclopedia Africana refers to the project W.B. Dubois was working on at his death: An encyclopedia of world Black culture.

P. 44 *A Love Supreme* is a song by John Coltrane. Philip Guston is an American painter.

P. 44 The Good Humor Man is an NYC ice cream vendor.

P. 46 Robert Desnos is a French surrealist poet. Suarez refers to the Spanish director Carlos Suarez. Frank Stanford is an American surrealist poet. Dolphy is jazz musician Eric Dolphy.

P. 49 French Philosophers Jacques Derrida and Emmanuel Levinas. A line from an unidentified poem by Gerald Stern.

P. 50 The narrative about "housewife," riffs the economic historical argument of Angela Davis.

P. 52 Sundiata refers to and quotes the great Mali Epic by that name.

P. 54 Roque Dalton, El Salvadoran poet. "All bourgeois poetry:" Haitian poet Jacques Romain riffing Leon Trotsky.

About The Author

Nationally reknowned performance poet Sean Thomas Dougherty was born in New York City in 1965. He grew up in an inter-racial family in predominately blue collar neighborhoods. He is a former factory worker and high school dropout. He has performed at colleges and performance venues across North America including the Connecticut Poetry Festival, the Detroit Art Festival, the Paterson Poetry Marathon, the Lollapalooza Music Festival, Los Angeles' Beyond Baroque, and Carnegie Mellon University. He is also the author of five books and an audio tape including *Except by Falling*, winner of the 2000 Pinyon Press Poetry Prize from Mesa State College. Dougherty's collaborative-installation on the life of Saint Catherine of Siena with Ecuadorian sculptor Larissa Marangoni premiered at Hallwalls Gallery in Buffalo, NY, and was shown at Fairfield U, and Providence College, resulting in the book *The Mercy of Sleep* (1995 Basfal) introduced by Christopher Buckley.

Dougherty's work appears in numerous anthologies and textbooks including *American Diaspora: Poets on Exile* (2001 U Iowa Press), *American Poetry: Next Generation* (2000 Carnegie Mellon U Press), *Identity Lessons* (1999 Viking Penguin), and *Poetry Nation* (1999 Vehicule, Canada). His awards include the Delmore Schwartz Poetry Prize, the U Mass Lowell Poetry Prize, the Syracuse Symposium Poetry Prize, and seven Pushcart Prize Nominations. He is the editor of CLMP Award winning *Red Brick Review*. He teaches at Penn State Erie.